$TOCK
ANALYSIS
101

A STEP BY STEP GUIDE TO
ANALYZING AND **BUYING** STOCKS

MABEL A. NUÑEZ, MBA
FOUNDER & CIO GIRL$ ON THE MONEY

I would like to thank my amazing book editor, Mrs. Charity Walton, for her time and dedication in helping me make this book the best it could possibly be. Charity was patient, diligent, and a true experienced professional. You can reach her at charity@goodshepherdpublications.com.

Special thank you to my friend and talented photographer, Yaritza Gonzalez for taking the photo you see on the backcover of this book. You can reach Yaritza on Instagram at @Yaryincharge

DEDICATION:

This book is dedicated first of all to God—for being my business partner and my guide in this wonderful journey. To my parents and sister, Alberto Nunez, Delsi Suriel, and Marlenne Nunez for always believing in me. To my nephews Derek and James for bringing so much joy into my life. I also dedicate this book to everyone in the **Girl$ on The Money** community for supporting my work and allowing me to teach investing for a living—a topic I am extremely passionate about. This is truly a gift I am grateful for every day. Thank you!

Introduction

Doing Your Research is Essential

"Investing without research is like playing stud poker and never looking at the cards."
-Peter Lynch

HELLO, FUTURE INVESTOR!

First of all, I want to thank you for investing in this guide. I am not just talking about the money, but about the **time** you will be investing in reading this. My #1 mission with this guide is that the knowledge you gain helps you make educated investment decisions that also turn profitable in the long term.

The finance media—television, radio, articles—are often filled with minute-by-minute coverage of the stock market that is often exaggerated and alarming. Enough to instill panic in people and scare them off from investing as a whole.

I want you to know that the media is doing its job, but it fails to provide a realistic view of what investing in **quality** and for the **long term** is all about.

The stock market is not a casino or a trip to Vegas. You won't make thousands of dollars in two hours or become rich overnight. You also don't have to sit in front of your computer for 7½ hours per day making investing decisions based on patterns on a chart. That strategy is a short-term approach called day trading, based on technical analysis, and is something that I find extremely risky.

This guide is based on **fundamental analysis**—a strategy followed by great investors of all-time including Warren Buffett, Benjamin Graham, and Peter Lynch, just to name a few. It is based on learning how to analyze stocks on your own so that you are able to make **educated** investment decisions, build a **diversified** portfolio of quality investments, and are able to create **wealth** over time.

And finally, I want to mention that I might use the names of real public companies from time to time throughout this guide. Keep in mind none of the stocks I mention are ever recommendations. They are used for educational purposes only and to bring a point across. Never invest or cease to invest based solely on the information provided.

I firmly believe in this saying: "Give a man a fish, and he will eat for a day. Teach a man to fish, and he will eat for a lifetime." Always do your own due diligence.

I wish you Health, Happiness, Success, and a whole lot of Profits!

Let's do this!

With gratitude,

Mabel A. Nunez, MBA

Table of Contents

Before we get started ...

INVESTING IS ONE of the most incredible and efficient ways in which you can put your money to work. If you are strategic about where you put your money, build a diversified portfolio of high-quality stocks, and allow your money time to grow and compound—the returns can be quite impressive and exciting.

With that said, nothing in life is "free," and that includes the market returns. The reason why investing can be such a fruitful endeavor is because there is also a higher level of risk involved in comparison to just having your money sitting in a savings account.

Before you start your investing journey, it is crucial to understand the risks that come with stock investing.

Below I share a few:

#1. When you buy an individual stock, you are buying part ownership of a company—this means that the return on your investment correlates to the performance of that company. When you buy a piece of business through stock investing, you are entrusting management to do everything in their power to make the company great and make sure your investment grows over time. You also go in with the agreement that there are no guarantees.

#2. Bad things can happen to great companies at any time. Companies go out of business, get disrupted by technology, lose their competitive advantage, and the list goes on. One way to protect your portfolio from crashing when a stock is doing poorly is to make sure you strategically diversify the investments you own. Also, make sure you are investing in quality. It is VERY dangerous to invest in random businesses you don't understand much about with the hope of just making a "quick buck."

#3. The market is unpredictable and volatile in the short term. It can go up or down at any time for any reason. You have to be able to put up with these kinds of "mood swings." The money you set aside to invest should be part of your disposable income—extra money you won't need for a while—at least the next 3-5 years. Money that you need for your emergency fund, your mortgage, your rent, your car payments, upcoming education expenses, anything immediate should **not** be in the stock market.

#4. Historically, the market has gone through severe crashes. You have to understand that those things happen, but you also have to know how to remain calm and remember that panicking is not an investing strategy. Some of the most notable market crashes include: Market crash of 1929, Black Monday (1987), the Dot Com Bubble of 2000, Housing Market Collapse of 2008. I lived through the market crash of 2008 and my enthusiasm for investing remained intact. Mostly because I understood from early on that fluctuations are a natural part of the investing cycle.

#5. If you invest blindly in anything that you don't understand just because of other people's recommendations, or simply because you think someone gave you a "hot stock tip," you dramatically increase the risk of losing your money very rapidly. Understand that investing is not playing the lottery. You MUST take the time to educate yourself, and this is something I will strive to help you with through the content I share in this guide, as well as all my educational resources.

In conclusion, investing is an incredible way to build wealth, but you have to learn to make educated decisions and understand that not all companies make great investments. I hope this guide provides you with the tools you need to make you more knowledgeable and confident about investing and helps you kick off your investing journey.

Let's get started!

Part I:
Analyzing an Individual Stock

(Fundamentals)

*"I can't emphasize enough
how important research is.
If you plan to buy stocks
solely based on what someone
told you to do or something you see in
an email or website but
fail to do your own research,
you run the risk of losing a
lot of money really fast."*

Step #1

Find Out if the Company is Publicly Traded

THE VERY FIRST THING you should understand is that there is a difference between a private company and a publicly traded company. When a company is private—the only people that have access to shares of the business are institutional investors, angel investors, or financial institutions that are willing to fund the growth of the business before shares of the company become available to the public.

When a company offers shares of stock to the public for the very first time, it is what we refer to as an IPO or "Initial Public Offering." Once an IPO is offered, it means the company is officially publicly traded, and the average person can now buy shares of the stock.

Finding out whether a company is publicly traded is relatively easy. A simple Google search can do the trick. **For example:**

"Is [company name] a publicly traded company?"

If the company is publicly traded, you'll notice tons of results including stock symbols and charts, and/or articles that confirm it.

If the company is still private, however, you might notice there are no stock charts or symbols. Instead, you might see an article or two that emphasize the company is private—which, as noted, means you cannot buy stock in it, and in that case, your research ends there.

Another thing you might notice while looking into this is that the company you are researching might have a parent company. In other words, it falls under the umbrella of a larger business. Which means you'll need to switch gears in your research and start looking up information on the parent company.

For example, let's say you really love Instagram and start to wonder whether it would be a good investment. As you conduct your research, you will soon notice that the parent company of Instagram is Facebook and therefore, your research going forward will need to be focused on Facebook, not Instagram.

Or, let's say you love Oreo cookies. As you start your research you'll soon notice that the parent company of Oreo is called Mondelez International.

These are just a couple of general examples to make you aware of this. Many brands that we know and recognize might have parent companies. This is an important factor to keep in mind as you conduct your research.

Find the Ticker Symbol

Now, let's say you confirm that the company is public and you can buy some stock in it if you wanted to, a quick action step you can take before moving into Step #2 is to find the company's Ticker Symbol.

The ticker symbol is just the name the stock of a company is given in the stock market. Sometimes it might look like the abbreviation of a company's name, but it is not always the case. It can be a combination of pretty much any letters chosen by the company. Knowing this information can help move through your research quicker and avoid confusion.

Finding the ticker symbol for any publicly traded company is very easy. You can just Google the phrase "what is the ticker symbol for [company name]" or go to a site like Google Finance {https://www.google.com/finance}, type in the name of the company in the search bar and see what comes up.

Something to keep in mind is that, in your search, you might notice different "versions" of the ticker symbol. For example, many public U.S-based businesses trade in international stock exchanges such as London, Shanghai, Frankfurt, Europe, etc.

If you plan to buy stock in the U.S. with U.S. currency make sure you identify the U.S.-Specific ticker symbol. A quick way to confirm whether is U.S. based is by making sure you see either "NYSE" or "NASDAQ" next to the name. If you see anything else, it might be the foreign version of the stock or something that trades in unregulated markets.

You can think of the "NYSE" (New York Stock Exchange) or the "NASDAQ" as the "homes" chosen by the business to house the shares they'll have available for the public. It doesn't really mean much when it comes to the investment itself. Below I share some examples of popular public companies, the ticker symbol, and their respective "home."

Company	Ticker	Exchange
Apple	AAPL	NASDAQ
Amazon	AMZN	NASDAQ
Alphabet	GOOGL	NASDAQ
Mondelez	MDLZ	NASDAQ
Facebook	FB	NASDAQ
Disney	DIS	NYSE
MasterCard	MA	NYSE
Visa	V	NYSE
Coca Cola	KO	NYSE
Hershey	HSY	NYSE

Step #2:

Add the Company to Your Personal Watch List

For as long as I can remember, even before starting my investing journey, I enjoyed keeping track of prospective investments that would catch my attention, and that I wanted to do more research on. I learned very quickly that if I didn't write these things down, I would soon forget. So, if you don't have a watch-list where you are keeping track of prospective investments, the time is now.

Having a list will make your research more efficient and organized. It will also become beneficial when you actually start putting together your own personal portfolio of individual stocks.

You don't need to overthink this! You can keep it simple as you get started and then add more information as time goes by. Open an excel spreadsheet and save it as "Stock Watch-list." In the worksheet, have three columns—Name, Date, Reasons/Comments.

Name—the name of the company you plan to research further.

Date—the date in which you added the company to your watch-list

Reasons/Comments—why the company has caught your attention and why you feel it may be a good investment and/or any other information you want to keep in mind.

7

You can also keep track of your watch-list using a virtual online portfolio. Sites like Yahoo! Finance and Google Finance have a "My Portfolio" feature where you can add the companies you are watching including any additional data you want to keep track of.

Step #3:

Prepare to Kick off Your Research

I CAN'T EMPHASIZE ENOUGH how important research is. If you plan to buy stocks solely based on what someone told you to do or something you see in an email or website but fail to do your **own** research, you run the risk of losing a lot of money really fast.

Not only that, but you can also create a lot of headaches and anxiety for yourself, especially when whatever you bought isn't performing well and you are trying to figure out if you should sell it and move on or hold on.

In the steps (or chapters) that follow, I'll explain one by one some of the main factors I consider extremely important as you complete your stock research.

Grab a pen, paper, and allocate an hour or two per week to do this. Have your platforms and resources ready to go.

Some of the sites and resources I consider of very high quality for research purposes include:

#1. **Investors Relations**—Every single company that is publicly traded has an "Investors Relations" tab somewhere on their website. Within that tab, you'll be able to find pretty much everything you need to complete your research including but not limited to quarterly reports (10Q), Annual reports (10K), financials, dividend history information (where applicable), press releases on new and/or upcoming developments and the list goes on. Don't worry about having to spend weeks digging in there, I'll explain in the coming sections which parts you should be focusing on.

#2. Morningstar—This is another one of my favorite sites for stock research. What I like about Morningstar is that they present financials for pretty much every single public company, as well as other investment vehicles such as ETFs or Index Funds in a way that is organized and easy to read. You can check out data from various years side by side which makes research a whole lot quicker and efficient.

#3. Google or Yahoo! Finance—I mostly use these sites as "quick look up" tools when I want to see the price for a stock and/or get a quick glimpse at profitability or valuation metrics such as the P/E or EPS, respectively. I'll talk more about valuation and financials in part II of this guide which is the Financial Health section.

Note on Google/Yahoo: Be cautious of "sponsored" articles presented in these sites as they can pretty much come from anywhere. The information might be too biased and fail to present an independent view. I instead rely on more "reputable" sources to get information in regard to the markets on any stock in particular. And that brings me to…

#4. Credible and Reputable Periodicals—If I come across any news by a publicly traded company while browsing the internet, I make sure to go onto one of my trusted sources to confirm whether the story is true or not. These mostly include:

- The Wall Street Journal

- Bloomberg (Online portal and Bloomberg Radio)

- The New York Times business section

- The Washington Post

- Reuters Business & Finance section

I probably don't have to tell you that there is a lot of fake news out there and it is difficult to decipher what's credible and what isn't. So, when it comes to investing, the quality of my sources is paramount. I recommend you adopt a similar strategy and are picky with your sources. As one of my favorite personal development Gurus, Mr. John Maxwell once said: "WHO you learn from is just as important as WHAT you learn."

Now that I've shared some of my top recommended sources for stock research, let's go into some of the prime factors you should consider as you evaluate a prospective investment.

Step #4:

Take a Close Look at Competition and Switching Costs

COMPETITION CAN BE a dangerous thing especially in the world of investing. It is very difficult for business, perhaps nearly impossible, to avoid competition of some kind. However, when the number of companies doing the exact same thing starts to get a bit overwhelming—I take that as a HUGE red flag.

Most of my portfolio is composed of influential leaders in various industries across the board. If I am invested in a particular company and see a lot of "copycats" emerging out of nowhere, and notice that the costs for a consumer to switch are low—that is usually a warning sign.

Companies in retail, telecommunication services, or streaming services make me nervous. The risk comes when a company is a pure play in the said industry—meaning that they only have one source of revenue that comes from products or services where competition is fierce. It gets even more dangerous when a consumer can quickly move from one company to another depending on who gives them the lowest price or the best deal.

Examples of companies that I personally believe fall into those "risky" categories include—meal kit services, music streaming services, phone service companies, and even some TV streaming services. Can you think of other examples?

Before you even consider investing in a company from an industry where competition is fierce, ask yourself the following questions:

#1 Is the company recognized as the leader in the industry in which it operates and has most of the market share or a significant portion of it?

#2 Is it too inconvenient and/or almost impossible for a consumer to switch?

#3 Does the company have multiple sources of income?

If the answer to two or more of these questions is "NO" you should ask yourself what exactly makes that business special (if anything) and whether it would make a good investment after all.

In a nutshell—I try to stay away from any kind of business where the customer's primary concern is to find the cheapest option, and there is no brand loyalty, moat, or competitive advantage.

Step #5:

Strategies For The Future

IF YOUR GOAL is to build a healthy stock portfolio of high-quality businesses that you plan to hold on to for many years going forward, you want to take a very close look at the plans the company has to stay relevant and ahead of the game in comparison to similar companies in the same industry.

Part of this analysis is looking at whether or not the products or services being offered by this company can be easily disrupted by another business or whether it is strong enough, and is being kept relevant enough, to fight off brewing competitors.

One quick way to learn more about the strategies, as well as current, ongoing, and future projects the business has, is by pulling up the annual report (10K) and taking a look under the **"Business"** section which is usually under **Item 1.**

You can find a company's most recent 10K by doing a quick Google search: "[Company name] annual report" or by going to the company's official website, clicking on the "investors" or "investors relations" tab and finding the link for annual reports.

Once you pull up the most recent annual report, you can find the business section by doing a quick look up on your desktop computer CTRL+F (PC) or Command+F (Mac) and typing in "Item 1. Business." You can also find it quickly in the table of contents:

Once you've located the business section, you can learn more about the company including other businesses it might have under its umbrella, as well as how it makes money. Many companies also include "strategies"—present and future—and this is where you can learn more about how a company plans to stay competitive.

15

Another way you can learn more about projects and strategies within the Investors or Investors Relations tab is by looking for the "Press Releases" link. This is where companies announce up-and-coming initiatives and business plans.

Questions you can ask yourself as you learn more about company strategies include:

- Can this company be easily disrupted?

- Where do I see this company in 10 years?

- Is this company "Amazon Proof"?

Let's be honest—no one has a crystal ball when it comes to determining with 100% certainty what can happen to an individual stock—or any investment for that matter. If we could predict the future, we would all be billionaires.

However, part of your analysis should always include putting on your "investor hat" and thinking about whether a business will be able to sustain its strength and competitive advantage to be around and thriving for many years to come. Think about whether the company might just be a fad with no foundation—here today and gone tomorrow—or whether it is actually solid with staying power.

Step #6:

Get to Know the Management

Some of my favorite investments have ironically turned out to be from companies who remain founder-led for many years. This means that the person that came up with the idea of the business remains at the helm either as the official CEO, chairman, or just part of the leadership committee.

With that said, not all companies in my portfolio, or those that I consider of high quality in general, are founder-led. This will usually mostly depend on how long the business has been around.

As an investor, I believe it is essential to get familiar with who the leadership team of a company is. You want to know whether the current CEO is one that's been there for several years (even if he/she is not the founder) or someone that jumps from company to company every couple of years.

The point of this is that it is nice to know that whoever is at the helm has skin in the game, and it is not someone that merely decided to lead a business because of the paycheck attached to the job, but because they actually care to see it growing and thriving.

Here are some quick steps to research the people at the helm of the company you are analyzing as a prospective investment:

17

#1. Go to the company's official website and look for the "Investors" or "Investor's Relations" tab. Click on it.

#2. Once in the investor's page, look for the "Corporate Governance" tab.

Once in that tab, you can learn more about the current CEO and might even come across a letter to shareholders. If you click on "Our Board" or "Board of Directors" you can learn more about top executives, how long they've been working at the company, and their respective backgrounds.

If you are feeling "extra" motivated and want to get a feel for the personality of anyone you see on that page, you can do a quick YouTube search to see if they've done a recent talk or presentation.

Step #7:

Social Responsibility—
is This Important to You?

"Make your investments the best
representation for your future."
-David Gardner

FROM TIME TO TIME I get questions about "socially re-sponsible" investing so I wanted to make sure I included a chapter about this.

You might not realize that investing in a business is like "voting with your dollars" because you are betting on its continued growth and development. That said, some peo-ple might not feel comfortable putting their investing mon-ey in companies that might not align with their ideals.

While it might sometimes be straightforward to figure out whether or not a company aligns with what you believe in—i.e., tobacco companies, fast food businesses, oil com-panies, certain "toxic" cosmetic companies, etc.—it might not be as "obvious" for others.

Here is a quick way to look into whether a company you are analyzing is "Socially Responsible":

#1 Go to a company's official website and browse around—in recent times, most companies are getting into the habit of highlighting current or upcoming

19

socially responsible projects. If they are doing some-thing right—they'll want you to know about it.

#2 On the company's homepage look for tabs such as "Impact," "Sustainability," or similar wording. It might vary from company to company, but if they are taking steps toward being socially responsible you best believe it will be on their site.

and/or

#3 You can just do a quick Google Search: "[Company Name] Sustainability Initiatives."

For the 3rd option—be very careful as you complete your search and always check your sources. You don't want to condemn a business you are interested in because you come across some questionable—perhaps fake—news, or vice versa. You also want the sources to be independent enough to help you reach your own conclusions.

Part II:
Analyzing an Individual Stock

(Financial Health)

*When you are examining a
company's financials,
you'll need to take a look
at the top financial statements
including the Balance Sheet,
the Income Statement, and
The Statement of Cash Flows.
But, don't worry—this is not
an accounting textbook.*

Step #8:

Find Out if the Company is Financially Healthy

BUSINESSES ARE JUST LIKE PEOPLE—when financials are healthy and thriving, they have the freedom and flexibility to invest in new products and services, venture out into various initiatives, and grow without the burden of massive debts and/or financial difficulties.

When you are examining a company's financials, you'll need to take a look at the top financial statements including the Balance Sheet, the Income Statement, and The Statement of Cash Flows. But, don't worry—this is not an accounting textbook.

While we can spend several pages of this book going over the lines of each financial statement one by one—this is not something I personally do in my investing research and also something I don't consider necessary.

Below I will share some of the top financial metrics I examine while completing research for a particular stock. Please note that you can easily find this information in a company's 10K (annual report) or in a site like Morningstar, as I shared earlier. Here is what you'll need to complete an intelligent analysis:

#1. About 5-10 years worth of data—this is important to make comparisons and look at trends over time. Don't worry about having piles of documents to look over. Five to ten years of financial data can be easily examined by pulling two to three of the most recent annual reports of a company and/or looking at the metrics on a site like Morningstar.

For example, let's say you want to take a peek at a company's financials over the past 10 years using the annual report (10K). Let's say the latest annual report available is from 2018. You'll pull reports from 2018 and 2017 for 10 years worth of data. Most single 10Ks will give about 5 years worth of financial information.

#2. A solid understanding of what the numbers mean and how to read the information (I'll explain that under each section).

#3. Your investor hat! Prepare to think like an investor. As one of my favorite investors Mr. Peter Lynch once said: "If you made it through fifth-grade math, you can do it!"

Let's do it!

Sales (Revenue) also referred to as "top line"

Sales, revenue, or "top line"—all the same thing—simply refers to how much money a company is generating from the products and/or services it sells. This is the number at the "very top" before any expenses, taxes, or deductions of any kind come into play.

The quickest way to find it:

Find the most recent annual report (also known as **10K**) **for the company:** This can be done through a quick Google search: "[Company Name] annual report." From the list that comes up, find the most recent report. Another way to find it is by going to the company's official website and clicking on the "Investors" or "Investors Relations" tab. Once in there, search around for "Annual Reports."

The cover page for most 10K's is standard and looks like this:

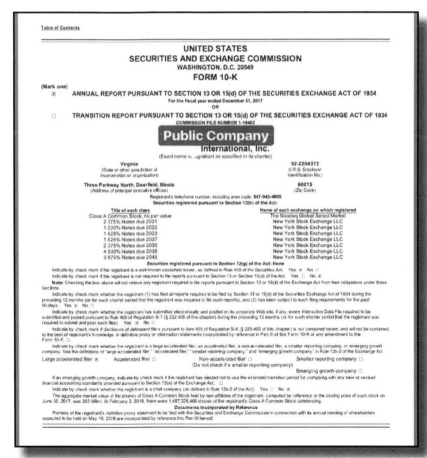

Locate the financial data within the report:

Once you open the most recent annual report, use CTRL+F on your keyboard (for PCs) or Command + F (for Mac) and type in **"Item 6. Selected Financial Data"** in the search tab. You can also just find Item 6 in the table of contents and click on it. Revenue should be the first line within that section: (**page 27**)

How to understand the numbers:

Most annual reports will give you about five years worth of financial data (side by side). Start with the oldest year available and work your way up to the most recent year.

As you compare, you want to make sure that sales have been going up consistently over time. If sales for a business you are interested in have been going down year over year, this could be a huge *red flag.* If sales have been inconsistent but seem to be gaining traction over the past few years, I'd take this as a positive sign. You always want to focus on TRENDS over time.

Net Income (Earnings) also known as "profits"

Net Income, earnings, or profits are all the same. They tell you how much money a company has left over after main expenses have been deducted. There is no reason to get overly technical with this. If a company makes $100 in sales, and it cost them $45 to create the products or services they sell, the net income (profit) is $55.

Item 6.   Selected Financial Data

Public Company
International, Inc. iational, Inc.
Selected Financial Data – Five Year Review (1)

	2017	2016	2015	2014	2013
		(in millions, except per share and employee data)			
Continuing Operations (2)					
Net revenues	$ 25,896	$ 25,923	$ 29,636	$ 34,244	$ 35,299
Earnings from continuing operations, net of taxes	2,936	1,669	7,291	2,201	2,332
Net earnings attributable to ▮▮▮:					
Per share, basic	1.93	1.07	4.49	1.29	1.30
Per share, diluted	1.91	1.05	4.44	1.28	1.29
Cash Flow and Financial Position (3)					
Net cash provided by operating activities	2,593	2,838	3,728	3,562	6,410
Capital expenditures	1,014	1,224	1,514	1,642	1,622
Property, plant and equipment, net	8,677	8,229	8,362	9,827	10,247
Total assets	63,109	61,538	62,843	66,771	72,464
Long-term debt	12,972	13,217	14,557	13,821	14,431
Total ▮▮▮ shareholders' equity	26,111	25,161	28,012	27,750	32,373
Shares outstanding at year end (4)	1,488	1,528	1,580	1,664	1,705
Per Share and Other Data					
Book value per shares outstanding	17.55	16.47	17.73	16.68	18.99
Dividends declared per share (5)	0.82	0.72	0.64	0.58	0.54
Common Stock closing price at year end	42.80	44.33	44.84	36.33	35.30
Number of employees	83,000	90,000	99,000	104,000	107,000

The quickest way to find it:

Following the same instructions as noted above, find "**Item 6. Selected Financial Data**" in the most recent annual report. Once in that section, look for Net Income/Earnings which will be somewhere under revenue. (**page 29**)

How to understand the numbers:

Same as you did when examining sales numbers—you want to make sure that Net Income has been going up consistently over time. If net income for a business you are interested in has been going down year over year, this could be a *red flag*. If net income has been inconsistent but seems to be gaining traction over the past few years, I'd take this as a positive sign. You always want to focus on TRENDS over time.

If you notice a significant outlier such as net income too high or low in a particular year in comparison to the others, it can mean the company went through a "special event" during that year—the merger or sale of a division, an acquisition, or something of the sorts.

Remember that one single year or one single quarter is not enough to make solid investing decisions. Focus on overall trends over time.

$ $ $

Long-Term Debt

Debt is self-explanatory. It tells you how much the company owes its creditors, vendors, private investors, whoever

Item 6.   Selected Financial Data

Public Company
International, Inc. rational, Inc.
Selected Financial Data – Five Year Review (1)

	2017	2016	2015	2014	2013
		(in millions, except per share and employee data)			
Continuing Operations (2)					
Net revenues	$ 25,896	$ 25,923	$ 29,636	$ 34,244	$ 35,299
Earnings from continuing operations, net of taxes	2,936	1,669	7,291	2,201	2,332
Net earnings attributable to ⁞					
Per share, basic	1.93	1.07	4.49	1.29	1.30
Per share, diluted	1.91	1.05	4.44	1.28	1.29
Cash Flow and Financial Position (3)					
Net cash provided by operating activities	2,593	2,838	3,728	3,562	6,410
Capital expenditures	1,014	1,224	1,514	1,642	1,622
Property, plant and equipment, net	8,677	8,229	8,362	9,827	10,247
Total assets	63,109	61,538	62,843	66,771	72,464
Long-term debt	12,972	13,217	14,557	13,821	14,431
Total ▉ shareholders' equity	26,111	25,161	28,012	27,750	32,373
Shares outstanding at year end (4)	1,488	1,528	1,580	1,664	1,705
Per Share and Other Data					
Book value per shares outstanding	17.55	16.47	17.73	16.68	18.99
Dividends declared per share (5)	0.82	0.72	0.64	0.58	0.54
Common Stock closing price at year end	42.80	44.33	44.84	36.33	35.30
Number of employees	83,000	90,000	99,000	104,000	107,000

lent the company money for business purposes. When examining financials, you might notice Short-Term Debt and Long-Term Debt. As investors, we mostly focus on Long Term Debt since this is the debt that will stick around with a business for *longer* than one year. Short-term debt is debt that the company can eliminate in a year or less.

The quickest way to find it:

Using the latest annual report of the company you are analyzing, use CTRL+F on your keyboard (for PCs) or Command+F (for Mac) and type in **"Item 6. *Selected Financial Data"*** in the search tab. Once in that section, find the line for "Long-Term Debt." **(page 31)**

How to understand the numbers:

What you want to make sure of is that long-term debt has been going down or remained somewhat consistent over time. Obviously, if the debt has been consistently increasing and it is significantly more than cash (explained below) that could be a *red flag*.

If there is massive debt, think about whether this is justified by the company making investments in the business that could potentially turn profitable, or whether the mounting debt makes no sense.

Item 6. Selected Financial Data

Public Company
International, Inc- iational, Inc.
Selected Financial Data – Five Year Review (1)

	2017	2016	2015	2014	2013
			(in millions, except per share and employee data)		
Continuing Operations (2)					
Net revenues	$ 25,896	$ 25,923	$ 29,636	$ 34,244	$ 35,299
Earnings from continuing operations, net of taxes	2,936	1,669	7,291	2,201	2,332
Net earnings attributable to ▇:					
Per share, basic	1.93	1.07	4.49	1.29	1.30
Per share, diluted	1.91	1.05	4.44	1.28	1.29
Cash Flow and Financial Position (3)					
Net cash provided by operating activities	2,593	2,838	3,728	3,562	6,410
Capital expenditures	1,014	1,224	1,514	1,642	1,622
Property, plant and equipment, net	8,677	8,229	8,362	9,827	10,247
Total assets	63,109	61,538	62,843	66,771	72,464
Long-term debt	12,972	13,217	14,557	13,821	14,431
Total ▇ shareholders' equity	26,111	25,161	28,012	27,750	32,373
Shares outstanding at year end (4)	1,488	1,528	1,580	1,664	1,705
Per Share and Other Data					
Book value per shares outstanding	17.55	16.47	17.73	16.68	18.99
Dividends declared per share (5)	0.82	0.72	0.64	0.58	0.54
Common Stock closing price at year end	42.80	44.33	44.84	36.33	35.30
Number of employees	83,000	90,000	99,000	104,000	107,000

Cash/Short-Term Investments

This is a liquidity metric which tells us how much money (or lack thereof) a company has in cash and/or in assets that can be quickly turned into cash if the company needs it.

You can think of this as the money an individual might have in a savings account. When it comes to the cash metrics, I like to look at the following:

- Cash & Cash Equivalents

- Cash generated by operating activities

- Free Cash Flow

- Net cash

The quickest way to find it:

Find the latest annual report (10K) of the company you are analyzing, use CTRL+F on your keyboard (for PCs) or Command+F (for Mac) and type in *"Consolidated Statement of Cash Flows"* in the search tab. You can also search the table of contents of the 10K for the same noted phrase. The actual report looks like this (**page 33**):

Once in that section, find the line for "Cash and cash equivalents" (usually toward the bottom of the statement, see arrow above).

You might also notice that instead of five years worth of data, you'll only get three years. If interested in the full five years, you might need to pull the second to last annual report as well.

For items like "Net Cash," you can do a quick search—use CTRL+F on your keyboard (for PCs) or Command+F (for Mac) and type in "net cash." Some companies will offer you comprehensive information all about liquidity and the net cash available year over year.

How to understand the numbers:

What you want to make sure of is that cash has been going up consistently over time. If cash for a business you

FINDING CASH AND SHORT TERM INVESTMENTS—EXAMPLE

▓▓▓▓▓▓, and Subsidiaries
Consolidated Statements of Cash Flows
For the Years Ended December 31
(in millions of U.S. dollars)

	2017	2016	2015
CASH PROVIDED BY/(USED IN) OPERATING ACTIVITIES			
Net earnings	$ 2,936	$ 1,669	$ 7,291
Adjustments to reconcile net earnings to operating cash flows:			
Depreciation and amortization	816	823	894
Stock-based compensation expense	137	140	136
U.S. tax reform transition tax	1,317	--	--
Deferred income tax benefit	(1,206)	(141)	(30)
Asset impairments and accelerated depreciation	334	446	345
Loss on early extinguishment of debt	11	428	748
Loss on deconsolidation of Venezuela	--	--	778
Gains on divestitures and JDE coffee business transactions	(186)	(9)	(6,822)
JDE coffee business transactions currency-related net gains	--	--	(436)
Gain on equity method investment transactions	(40)	(43)	--
Equity method investment net earnings	(460)	(301)	(56)
Distributions from equity method investments	152	75	58
Other non-cash items, net	(225)	(43)	199
Change in assets and liabilities, net of acquisitions and divestitures:			
Receivables, net	(24)	31	44
Inventories, net	(18)	62	(49)
Accounts payable	5	409	659
Other current assets	14	(176)	28
Other current liabilities	(637)	60	152
Change in pension and postretirement assets and liabilities, net	(333)	(592)	(211)
Net cash provided by operating activities	2,593	2,838	3,728
CASH PROVIDED BY/(USED IN) INVESTING ACTIVITIES			
Capital expenditures	(1,014)	(1,224)	(1,514)
Proceeds from JDE coffee business transactions currency hedge settlements	--	--	1,050
Acquisitions, net of cash received	--	(246)	(527)
Proceeds from divestitures, net of disbursements	604	303	4,735
Reduction of cash due to Venezuela deconsolidation	--	--	(611)
Capital contribution to JDE	--	--	(544)
Proceeds from sale of property, plant and equipment and other assets	109	138	60
Net cash (used in)/provided by investing activities	(301)	(1,029)	2,649
CASH PROVIDED BY/(USED IN) FINANCING ACTIVITIES			
Issuances of commercial paper, maturities greater than 90 days	1,808	1,540	613
Repayments of commercial paper, maturities greater than 90 days	(1,911)	(1,031)	(710)
Net issuances/(repayments) of other short-term borrowings	1,027	1,741	(931)
Long-term debt proceeds	350	5,640	4,624
Long-term debt repaid	(1,470)	(6,186)	(4,975)
Repurchase of Common Stock	(2,174)	(2,601)	(3,622)
Dividends paid	(1,198)	(1,094)	(1,008)
Other	207	129	126
Net cash used in financing activities	(3,361)	(1,862)	(5,883)
Effect of exchange rate changes on cash and cash equivalents	89	(76)	(255)
Cash and cash equivalents:			
(Decrease)/increase	(980)	(129)	239
Balance at beginning of period	1,741	1,870	1,631
Balance at end of period	$ 761	$ 1,741	$ 1,870
Cash paid:			
Interest	$ 398	$ 630	$ 747
Income taxes	$ 848	$ 527	$ 745

See accompanying notes to the consolidated financial statements.

are interested in has been decreasing year over year, that is a *red flag*—especially if it gets to the point where debt is aggressively increasing, and cash is aggressively going the other way.

Step #9:

Look into Profitability and Valuation Metrics

Earnings per Share (EPS)

Earnings per Share is the leading indicator of profitability used by most analysts and investors. It measures how much profit the company is generating *per each individual share of common stock* that is available to the public (also known as "The Float"). Generally speaking, the higher the EPS number, the higher the company's profit per share.

EPS is useful to make year over year, and/or quarter over quarter, comparisons to see if the company's profitability is increasing or decreasing over time. Because of this, it is one of the most popular metrics looked at by Wall Street analysts whenever a company reports earnings.

The quickest way to find it:

For company-specific EPS, you can go to a site like morningstar.com and find the specific page for the company you are analyzing by typing in the name in the search tab. Remember to make sure you see "NYSE" or NASDAQ" next to the company name or ticker symbol, which is the US-Based version of the stock.

Once in the stock-specific page, search the page until you find the **"Key Ratios"** tab then click on it.

Once on the ratios page, search for the **"Earnings Per Share"** line on the left-hand side. Note that you might need to click on "Full Ratios Data" to see everything.

How to understand the numbers:

A site like Morningstar might give you 5-10 years worth of data. Start by looking at the oldest year possible and work your way up to the latest year available. For example—let's say you are offered data ranging from 2008 to 2017—you would take a look at Earnings Per Share numbers year over year starting at 2008 through the most current year to see whether it has been increasing over time, decreasing, or whether it has remained somewhat consistent.

If the EPS seems to be *increasing* year over year, it generally means the profitability is increasing. If you noticed EPS has been *decreasing,* it could signal that the profitability is slowing, and this can be a *red flag*.

An important note on EPS analysis:

If you are analyzing a company and notice that the EPS in recent years is negative—this means the company is **NOT** profitable. Many people are under the impression it is okay to invest in an unprofitable business with the hope that "someday" the company will start making money and they'll be "ahead of the game."

However, putting money in businesses that are unprofitable is **VERY** risky and is something that I personally don't do.

One of my firm strategies when it comes to publicly traded companies is staying away from businesses that are not yet (or no longer) profitable.

A quick way to find this out is by looking at the most recent EPS or even P/E numbers. If that number is negative, just know that the business is not making a profit.

$$$

The Price to Earnings Ratio (P/E Ratio)

The P/E ratio is a valuation metric that tells you whether a particular stock is undervalued ("cheaper"), overvalued ("more expensive"), or fair, relative to the market as a whole or companies within the same industry.

The P equals the current market price per share of the stock while the E stands for the most recent earnings per share.

By dividing the price per share over the earning per share, we can determine whether the current price of the stock is fair considering the earnings the company is generating. It can also tell us whether the price is overvalued or undervalued, as initially noted.

Let's look at an example:

Let's say you are looking at two companies in the same industry. Company A has a price per share of $62 with a P/E of 40. Meanwhile, Company B has a price per share of $85 with a P/E of 10.

Although at first glance you might automatically think Company A is the "cheaper" stock, by valuation standards, Company B would be considered the cheapest option considering the lower P/E. The lower P/E can mean more potential for growth and signal a possibly undervalued stock.

Now, if we are comparing this to the market as a whole—let's say the S&P 500 (which is the index that represents the "market" in the U.S.) has a current P/E of 22.31. That means Company B is considered undervalued or "cheaper" in comparison to the market as a whole. Meanwhile, Company A is considered "overvalued" or more "expensive" relative to the market.

Please note P/E is <u>not</u> the only valuation metric, but one of the most commonly used standards for stock research. Also, I wouldn't use the P/E ratio as my **single** point of reference when deciding whether or not to invest in something. Investing is not an exact science. There are MANY companies out there with a P/E that might seem overly expensive, which have actually done very well for shareholders.

At the end of the day, it will depend on the business you are analyzing, and in taking a holistic view of the company as a whole as opposed to focusing on one single factor. P/E is only a piece of the puzzle in your overall stock research.

The quickest way to find it:

For the company-specific P/E ratio, you can go to a site like morningstar.com and find the specific page for the company you are analyzing by typing in the name in the search tab. Remember to make sure you see "NYSE" or NASDAQ" next to the company name or ticker symbol, which is the US-Based version of the stock.

Once in the stock-specific page, click on the *"valuation"* tab. On the left-hand side, look for "Price/Earnings." The most up to date P/E can be found under "Current."

On the very far right column you might also see "index" — which shows you at a glance where the company's valuation stands next to the market average.

When it comes to the P/E of various market indexes, including the S&P 500, my go-to-source is the Wall Street Journal P/E & Yields page. Once on that page, scroll down to where you see "other indexes" and look for the S&P 500. Once there, take a look at the P/E ratio number trailing over 12 months.

An important note on P/E analysis:

When a company has a high P/E it doesn't always mean the stock is "too expensive" and you should stay away or vice versa.

A high P/E could also be a reflection that the market has very high expectations for that company and expects a lot of growth and profitability *in the future*, and so it has a higher earnings multiple.

The opposite is also true for companies with P/E's that are low in comparison to the market as a whole, or other peers in its industry. A lower P/E may not necessarily mean the stock is a "great bargain;" it might also indicate the market has fewer expectations of that stock for future growth.

As always, it will all depend on the company you are analyzing and its future prospects. You can pair up your P/E analysis with how a company has been performing so far, and also its growth & profitability plans for the future.

Remember that the P/E ratio is only **one** tool, part of the "puzzle" of your comprehensive investing research.

$ $ $

The PEG Ratio

Definition:

The Price/Earnings to Growth (PEG) ratio is a valuation metric that can help you take your P/E analysis a step further. While a stock you are analyzing might seem undervalued or fairly valued by P/E standards, taking it a step further and looking at the PEG can help you strengthen your research.

The formula for PEG is made up of the current price of the stock over the company's earnings growth rate—which is calculated using the current year and prior year EPS numbers.

The quickest way to find it:

You can calculate the metric yourself or go to a site like morningstar.com. Find the specific page for the company you are analyzing by typing in the name in the search tab.

Remember to make sure you see "NYSE" or NASDAQ" next to the company name or ticker symbol, which is the US-Based version of the stock.

Once on the stock-specific page, click on the *"valuation"* tab. On the left-hand side, look for "PEG ratio." The most up to date P/E can be found under "Current."

How to use the information:

While the accuracy of the PEG ratio will depend on the type of company you are analyzing—the lower the PEG, the larger the potential for growth for the stock. Generally speaking, you want the PEG to be under one.

Remember this is not a rule and investing is not an exact science. You can use this analysis as part of the overall puzzle of your stock research.

$ $ $

The Forward Price to Earnings Ratio

The forward P/E is a profitability metric based on expectations for a particular stock. It is a prediction on potential future growth based on estimated data. The formula is composed of the current price of the stock over the estimated (or forecasted) earnings per share.

The forecasted earnings used in the formula can be for the next 12 months or for the next fiscal year period, and are usually a number agreed upon by Wall Street

Analysts based on historical data for the company, as well as expectations.

The quickest way to find it:

You can go to a site like morningstar.com and find the specific page for the company you are analyzing by typing in the name in the search tab. Remember to make sure you see "NYSE" or NASDAQ" next to the company name or ticker symbol, which is the US-Based version of the stock.

Once on the stock-specific page, click on the *"valuation"* tab. On the left-hand side, look for *"Price/Forward Earnings."* The most up to date Forward P/E can be found under "Current."

On the very far right column, you might also see "index" — which shows you, at a glance where the company's forward P/E valuation stands next to the market average.

How to use the information:

You can compare the forward P/E ratio of the stock with the current P/E ratio to determine what the analyst expectations are when it comes to growth potential. If the forward P/E is lower than the actual P/E, it means analysts expect earnings for the company to increase. Meanwhile, if the forward P/E is higher than the actual P/E, it means analysts expect earnings to decrease.

I want to make it clear that this is not a "rule" and investing is not an exact science. You can use this tool as a piece of the puzzle in your overall and comprehensive research of the stock.

$$\$\ \$\ \$$$

Operating Margin

The Operating Margin is a profitability metric.

The purpose of the margin is to give us an idea of how much money a company makes *(before interests and taxes)* on each dollar of sales. Generally speaking, the higher the operating margin the more profitable the company is.

You want operating margins to either be increasing over time or remaining somewhat consistent. You might notice that the operating margin for more mature businesses remains consistent year over year as opposed to showing aggressive growth.

The quickest way to find it:

For company-specific ratios, you can go to a site like morningstar.com and find the specific page for the company you are analyzing by typing in the name in the search tab. Remember to make sure you see "NYSE" or NASDAQ" next to the company name or ticker symbol, which is the US-Based version of the stock.

Once on the stock-specific page, find the *"Key Ratios"* tab and click on it.

Once on the ratios page, scroll down to find the **"Operating Margin %"** line. Note that you might need to click on "Full Ratios Data" to see everything.

How to understand the numbers:

Start by looking at the oldest year possible and work your way up the most recent year available. For example—let's say you are offered data ranging from 2008 to 2017. You would take a look at **Operating Margin** percentage numbers year over year, starting at 2008 and through current times to see whether the percentage has been increasing over time, decreasing, or whether it has remained somewhat consistent.

If you notice that the operating margin has been decreasing *significantly* over the years, this could be a *red flag* when it comes to the profitability of the business.

Example:

Let's say the current operating margin percentage of a company you are analyzing is at 15%. This means the business makes about $0.15 per each dollar of sales before it has to take care of core obligations including taxes and interest fees for any debts the company may have.

The higher that percentage, the better, because it means there is more money left over to pay obligations, invest back into the business, and distribute back to shareholders.

When making comparisons in stock research from one company to the next, it is better to compare businesses in the same industry or "apples-to-apples" for a more accurate assessment.

The operating margin of tech companies that focus on software, for example, might be much higher than that of a company that actually makes physical products. Part of this is because it costs more to produce tangible goods as opposed to intellectual property. It might have nothing to do with the respective profitability of each stand-alone business.

Part III:
Buying Your First Individual Stock

(And Beyond!)

When you are investing
for the long term—
years not days—
temporary fluctuations
in the markets should
be expected and not
cause unnecessary panic.

Step #1:

Choose Your Platform of Choice

When I first started my investing journey—back in the summer of 2008—the options we had for buying or selling stocks were minimal. We could either go to a bank, open an investing account, hire a money manager, and then hope for the best.

Or, we could buy and sell our investments through something called an "online broker." This is an option that, thankfully, we still have today.

Examples of popular online brokers in recent times include, but are not limited to:

1. Ally Invest

2. TD Ameritrade

3. E*Trade

4. Merrill Edge

5. Charles Schwab

Among many others!

Depending on the year in which you are reading this, you can find reviews for the best online brokers available by doing a simple Google search. Example: "Best online brokers of [insert year]." Websites such as NerdWallet, Magnify Money, and The Ascent by the Motley Fool do a great job providing reviews which can be very helpful as you narrow down your options.

When choosing an online broker, here are some important factors to look into:

Is the broker SIPC/FINRA insured? This means that if anything happens to the online broker, the money you have in the account will be insured up to $500,000.

Note that these entities don't protect you when you lose money in your investments (that is your full responsibility) they simply protect your money if something happens to the online broker. This is similar to banks being FDIC insured.

Do they require an account minimum? Some investment accounts require a minimum dollar amount before you are able to open an account. However, most online brokers do not have any account minimum requirements. This means you can open an investment account with whatever dollar amount you can afford today and work your way up from there.

How much is the trading fee? Online brokers will charge you anywhere from $0 to $7.95 per trade depending on the broker. *I will elaborate more in the next sections on how this works.*

Today, in addition to those online brokers, we also have:

- Apps that invest for us (Acorns, Stash)
- Apps that allow you to invest on your own (Robinhood, M1 Finance)

- Robo advisors (Betterment, Wealthfront)

…and the list goes on!

The cool thing about having so many options is that a lot of the new "up and coming" platforms for investing are either free (which is the case with the apps) or have very low/reasonable commission fees.

For example, when using an online broker you can expect to pay anywhere from $4.95 to $7.95 per transaction every time you buy or sell stocks. Meanwhile, Robo Advisor management fees start at around 0.25% per year depending on which one you choose.

The "downside" of so many options is that it can get quite overwhelming and confusing. Here you are trying to figure out how to pick good investments, but also have to worry about which platform to go with. Feeling overwhelmed can be enough to leave you wondering whether investing is too "out of your league" and perhaps you should leave it alone.

However, not investing at all will seriously slow down your ability to create wealth over time (unless you win the lottery) and so, you SHOULD be investing.

To ease the confusion, in this section I'll be focusing on two of my favorite platforms for "do it yourself" investing:

1. Self-directed online brokers.

2. Apps that allow you to invest on your own.

Both of these options are self-directed accounts meaning that you'll be able to buy/sell stocks on your own. In the section where we talk about Apps, I'll also share some options that are more "hands-off" considering those are also very popular in this day and age.

Once you have selected an online broker (or an app), you'll also need to understand how to open one, fund it, and how to actually make investment transactions. In the following sections, I will explain all of that and more.

Let's get started!

Self-Directed Online Brokerage Account

We are kicking off the platform section with my old school favorite—an online brokerage account.

As previously noted, this applies to those of you that want to open an investment account that you can manage yourself and allows you to buy and sell stocks on your own.

In the sections where I explain how to buy or sell a stock, I will be using sample images from a specific broker for educational purposes and to explain how brokers work and what to expect. I've found that the platform for most online brokers look similar, have the same features, and allow you to do the same things. Hence, what you learn in this section should be applicable to any broker you choose.

Let's proceed with first steps.

Opening the account:

Go to the official website of the online broker of your choice and click on "Get Started" or "Open Account." Once you click on that, you might be presented with a couple of options: "Self-Directed Trading" or "Managed Portfolio."

If you plan to buy/sell stocks on your own, go with self-directed trading.

Managed portfolio means you want to hire someone at the online broker to invest on your behalf for a fee.

Once you make your selection, you'll need to choose which kind of account you want:

1. Individual Account

2. Joint Account

3. Traditional IRA

4. Roth IRA

5. Rollover IRA

6. UTMA/UGMA (custodial accounts)

Again, for the purpose of this guide, we are going with the **"Individual Account"** option. If you plan to open your investing account with a spouse, you can choose the **"Joint Account"** option, but make sure to read the requirements for that and whether you'll need authorization from the other party at all times before making any decisions in the account. This can make the process time consuming and cumbersome at times.

Remember there are other options you can choose from depending on the reasons why you are opening your account, but we are focusing on individual self-directed accounts in this book.

Once you make your selection on the type of account you want, you'll be asked a series of questions that will range from your name to your social security number. The application will look very familiar to what you fill out when applying for a credit card or a bank account.

Many people wonder why online brokers ask for your social security number. The reason is straightforward—they want to make sure you are not involved in any money laundering activities or trying to do anything illegal—plain and simple. The number is also needed for tax purposes.

All online brokers and investing accounts will ask for your social security number. Make sure that the company you go with for your investment account is one that is preferably well known and is insured by the SIPC and FINRA (you can quickly check for this in the Q&A section of any online brokerage account under "Account Protection" questions).

Funding the account:

Once the account is open, you'll need to fund it with some cash to start investing. The good news is that most online brokers have no minimum requirements. This means that you can fund it with $200, or $2,000, or whatever you can afford, as you begin your investing journey.

To make the transfer, you will notice the online broker will provide a few options. The simplest and most straightforward option is through an ACH Transfer. This allows you to link your online broker with your bank account of choice. To do this, you'll go through a few security steps. Once your checking account of choice is connected with your investing account, you can select the exact dollar amount you want to transfer for investing purposes.

You can also fund your investing account using a personal check. However, some online brokers charge a fee for this and the amount of time it'll take to fund your account will be longer.

Once you've allowed a transfer, some online brokers might have a three-day processing period before your money becomes available for investing purposes. Some, however, make the transferred funds available immediately. It will usually depend on the broker.

A word of caution—your emergency fund and your investment fund are two completely different things. Never transfer money you have saved for emergencies, or that you might need within the next 3–5 years, to an investing account.

The stock market is volatile and unpredictable in the short term. Anything can happen. You don't want to be caught in a situation where you fund your investing account with money you might need soon, and then something happens and you have to cash out prematurely.

Here's an example of an unfavorable scenario: Let's say the market is going through a downturn for any random reason and you need the money that you have in the account. Not only will you be forced to cash out—perhaps at a loss— but your investments will immediately miss the chance to continue growing and compounding over time.

The money you invest needs time to grow, compound, and recover from any unexpected volatility happening in the markets. This is why quality investing, diversification, and time go hand in hand.

What you should expect to pay:

When it comes to "self-directed" online brokerage accounts, there is no such thing as ongoing monthly fees or anything of the like. The only "expenses" you need to worry about are the transaction fees—how much you'll pay to buy and sell stocks and the taxes on your realized* gains and/or dividend payments when tax time rolls around.

Most popular online brokers today that have no minimum account requirements, will charge you anywhere from $4.95 to $7.95 per trade. How does this work? Very simple.

Using the $4.95 example—Let's say you want to purchase 10 shares of Company A all at once. You will pay $4.95 for the transaction. Let's say you decide to sell 5 of those shares (or your entire position of 10) in a few years, you'll be charged $4.95 again—as long as the transaction happens **all at once.**

Some people get confused thinking the fee is per share of stock, which is not the case. All costs are per transaction.

Let's say that instead, you want to buy 5 shares of Company A and 5 shares of Company B. In this case, you'll be charged $4.95 twice—once after each transaction—because you are purchasing two different stocks and two separate operations are taking place.

---

* *Taxes on realized capital gains (profits) will depend on a few factors including your tax bracket, whether you also sold at a loss, among other factors. You will receive a Form 1099 in the mail as a new tax season approaches. Make sure you bring the document to your tax preparer. We talk more about "realized" and "unrealized" gains or loses later in the guide.*

Steps to purchase a stock:

Before we get into the step-by-step process of purchasing a stock, I do want to note that transactions should ideally be completed during market hours which are 9:30 am to 4:00 pm EST Monday through Friday. Some people choose to invest before the market opens, after the market closes, or even on weekends. However, this is not a good idea and something I wouldn't recommend.

Not only do many online brokers charge you a higher fee for trading when the market is closed, but also the market is very illiquid when it's closed—meaning there are not many transactions taking place. You want to make sure you are buying or selling during the times that the market is officially in action.

With that said, let's walk through a real-life example of how to purchase a stock.

For most online brokers, this is what the transaction screen will look like (or very similar to this). (**page 60**)

To get to the screen where you buy or sell stocks, click on "Trading" *(circled)*. Then select the option for "Stocks & ETFs." The transaction page will look something like this (see page 61):

Although you see a whole lot of options presented in the transaction screen, which is where it can get confusing. Just forget about all the other tabs on top. We are keeping it simple and focusing on buying/selling stocks.

Make sure you are in the "stocks" tab (as pictured in the chart on **page 61**) and focus on the following selections:

Action: Buy **or** Sell

Shares: How many shares of the stock you want to buy

Symbol: The ticker symbol of the stock

Price: Choose the Limit **or** Market Order option (will explain on **page 62**)

Duration: Choose the Day Order **or** GTC option (will explain on **page 63**)

While **Action, Shares,** and **Symbol** are self-explanatory, here is a quick explanation:

Buy: Choose this option if you plan to buy stock(s).

Sell: Choose this option if you plan to sell stock(s).

Shares: The number of shares you plan to buy **or** sell

Symbol: The **ticker symbol** of the stock (or fund) you plan to buy or sell.

Price and **Duration** have options and here is what they mean:

Under price, you will notice multiple options. However, to make this as simple as possible and avoid confusion, I will explain what Market and Limit mean. You can select the

GETTING TO THE STOCK TRANSACTION SCREEN—EXAMPLE

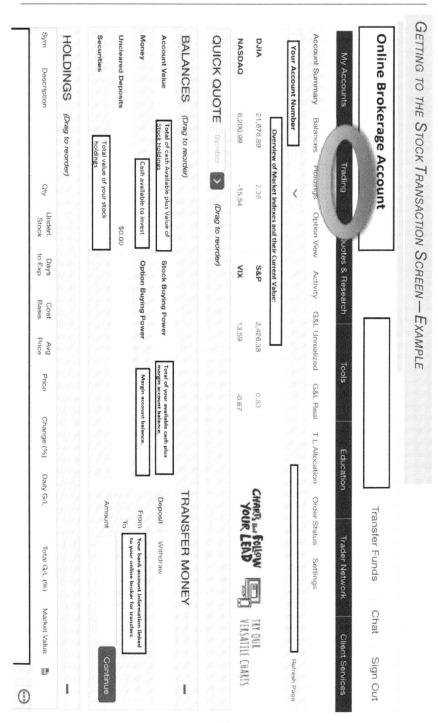

Understanding Market and Limit Orders—Example

| My Accounts | Quotes & Research | Trading | Tools | Education | Trader Network | Client Services |

Stocks + ETFs | Extra Hours | Basic | Covered Call | Protective Put | Collar | 2 Legs ▾ | 3 Legs ▾ | 4 Legs ▾ | Bulk | Order Status

60974276 - Individual Account ▾

As of: 02/06/15 11:07 AM ET | Print | Guide to use this page

U.S. Markets close in 4:50:06

Action
- ○ Buy
- ○ Sell
- ○ Sell Short
- ○ Buy to Cover

Shares

Symbol

🔍 Find Stock Symbol
Preferred Stock Format

Price
- ○ Market
- ● Limit
- ○ Stop
- ○ Stop Limit
- ○ Market on Close

Duration
- ● Day Order
- ○ GTC
- ⊞ Qualifiers

Advanced Orders: ▸ Disclaimer

one you feel more comfortable with when it comes time to make a stock purchase.

Market and **limit** are also the only two options I personally use.

Market means you want to buy the stock at the current market price—the price the stock is trading at during the time in which you are making the purchase. This is the simplest and most straightforward option if you just want to add a stock to your portfolio and are okay with the current price.

Limit means you want to **specify** the price at which you want the online broker to buy the stock for you. So, for example, let's say you want to purchase shares of a stock that is currently trading at $49 per share. However, you don't want to pay that much and want to buy the stock at $45 per share. By using limit and entering the dollar amount you want, you are telling the online broker to only complete the transaction IF the stock reaches that desired price.

The risk you run into with limit orders is that the stock you want might continue to go up in price. So, you might have to eventually cancel that specification and just buy the stock at whatever price it is. Also, it's important to note that if you plan to hold on to a particular stock for many years—and it actually turns out to be an excellent investment—whether or not you saved "$4" a few years ago might be irrelevant.

With that said, some people do feel more comfortable specifying a purchase price, and there is nothing wrong with that. The limit option allows for specifications.

When choosing "Limit," you'll also have the option to specify how long you want that order to stay active as you wait for a specific price. The specification is made under "Duration."

Under Duration, you'll notice two options: "Day Order" or "GTC."

Day Order means you want the online broker to keep your specification active just for that trading day. That means that if the stock doesn't go to your desired price of $44 per share (using the example I gave earlier) on that same day, the online broker will cancel the order at the end of the trading day which is 4:00 PM EST.

GTC means "Good Until Cancelled" and tells the online broker to keep the price specification active until you personally cancel it. The default GTM for most online brokers is about 60 days, but you are usually provided with a list of options and can specify your own time frame.

What happens next?

Once you complete the transaction screen with your selections, you'll notice a "Preview Order" tab somewhere toward the bottom of the page which will allow you to take a closer look at your transaction before it actually goes through. Make sure you review this **VERY** closely before clicking "Confirm" on your order.

In addition to making sure you are buying the correct stock, you also want to make sure you have enough money in cash in your account to complete your requested transaction.

63

Once you click "confirm" you might notice your purchase request goes into a "pending orders" tab before the transaction officially goes through. Once the transaction takes place—**congratulations!** You are now an official part owner of the business.

I want to make an emphasis on making sure you have enough money in your investment accounts for every transaction that you make. While not required, I'd also recommend you have a cushion of money left over after every purchase, if possible.

If you try to make a transaction that turns out to cost more than the money you have available in your investing account, the broker "might" allow this to go through thanks to something called "Margin."

In simple terms, the broker will lend you money to invest, which is something I have personally never done and consider to be a very high risk, especially for beginners. I talk more about margin investing later in the book.

Investing Applications or "Apps"

When I first started my investing journey, apps were unheard of. However, things have changed drastically. Stock investing apps of all flavors imaginable have been emerging in the investing world over the past several years. You can choose from a variety of options ranging from Apps that are more "hands-off", meaning, they invest on your behalf, as well as those that are more "hands-on" and allow you full control over your investments—similar to an online broker.

There are many investing apps to choose from in current times. Some of the most popular ones include:

1. Robinhood

2. M1 Finance

3. Acorns

4. Stash

Among many others!

Apps like Robinhood and M1 Finance are more "hands-on" and will allow you to buy and sell individual stocks, as well as Exchange Traded Funds, all on your own.

Meanwhile, apps like Acorns and Stash are more "hands-off" and will **invest on your behalf** based on your risk tolerance and investing goals.

Depending on the year in which you are reading this, you can find the best investing apps available by doing a simple Google search. Example: "Best investing apps of [insert year]." Websites such as NerdWallet, Magnify Money, and The Ascent by the Motley Fool do a great job providing reviews which can be very helpful as you narrow down your options.

Let's take a look at some of your options.

Apps That Are More "Hands-On"—Allow you Full Control Over Your Investments

The apps we are covering in this section are those that work similar to an online brokerage account because they allow you full control over which stocks you can buy or sell.

While these apps are great for beginners or anyone that doesn't want to pay a fee to buy and sell stocks, you should be aware that these platforms do come with some limitations.

Most apps will only allow you to open a self-directed taxable account to buy and sell individual stocks and ETFs (Exchange Traded Funds). Most will not allow you to open other types of accounts or invest in other investment vehicles such as Index Funds.

This means that, unlike the online broker, if you wanted to buy an Index Fund or open an IRA, Roth IRA, a custodial account or any kind of account other than a self-directed taxable account, you wouldn't** be able to do so.

Another thing you should be aware of (and cautious of) with these kinds of apps is that, while they do not charge you any trading fees, they sometimes do make it "convenient" for individuals to invest on margin.

Investing on margin means you borrow money from the broker to invest, often at high-interest rates, which is a **terrible** idea—especially for a beginner. I have never invested on

---

** *The only exception I've come across when it comes to this is M1 Finance which does allow for someone to open different kinds of accounts.*

margin myself and it is not something I am a fan of. I elaborate more on what margin means later in the book.

As noted, example of apps that are free and allow you to make your own investment decisions include:

- Robinhood.

- M1 Finance.

Apps That Are More "Hands-Off"—Will Manage Investments For You:

These types of apps are also perfect for beginners and individuals that perhaps do not have the time, motivation, or patience to do the research and build an investment portfolio on their own. Also, for those of you that might not want the "responsibility" of selecting your own investments.

These apps allow you to be more "hands off" while still being able to send your money to "work".

Depending on the app—the way you can fund the account for investment purposes will vary. You can fund the account yourself, schedule automatic transfers, select to transfer your spare change, transferring $5 to start out and then at selected intervals, and the list goes on.

The point is that these apps have the goal of eliminating the "guesswork" that comes from how much to invest or when to invest and want to do it for you. This is after completing an initial questionnaire and scheduling preferred scheduled transfers.

When you first download the app into your phone, you'll be asked a series of questions which allow the platform to determine your risk tolerance—whether you are more conservative or are okay with "riskier" investments.

Based on your answers, your money is invested in different kinds of funds by something called an "algorithm." You can think of an algorithm as a type of Artificial Intelligence technology.

Please note that at the present time, these types of apps **do not** invest in individual stocks. They put your money in **funds** that are tailored to your specific risk tolerance. You will not have control over where your money is being invested as the funds are chosen by the app's algorithm, as noted.

An example of these kinds of apps as of this day and age include:

- Acorns.

- Stash.

This concludes our section on investing platforms. As you make a decision on which ones to go with, ask yourself these questions:

1. Do you want to be more **"hands-on"** plus also have the flexibility to opening an IRA and/or invest in ETFs and/or Index Funds in the future? In that case, online brokers are your best option.

2. Do you want to be more **"hands-on,"** like the idea of investing for free, and are only interested in stock investing? In this case, online brokers that allow you to invest on your own are your best bet.

3. Do you prefer to be more **"hands-off"** and have an algorithm choose investments on your behalf at very low fees? In that case robo-Advisors or Apps that invest on your behalf will be your best option.

And remember, there are other types of platforms out there. However, I am presenting you the simplest, most straight forward, option as you get started with your investing journey. There is no need to overcomplicate things. The choice is yours!

Step #2:

Understanding Unrealized vs. Realized Gains and Losses

Unrealized vs. Realized Gains

Now that we've discussed how to choose your investing platform and buy your first stock(s), it is essential you understand the differences between unrealized and realized.

There will be a tab within your investing account called the **"G&L Unrealized"** or something similar. It will look something like this: (**page 71**)

The "unrealized/realized" screen shows you how much money you have personally made or lost on a particular investment based on how much you paid for it.

Here is the important factor to understand: A gain (or loss) doesn't become "real" until you actually SELL something. You must actually go into the transaction screen (explained in the previous section) and complete a "sell" transaction for any gains or losses within your account to become realized or real.

Even if you notice you might be losing some money within your investing account on any given day—that doesn't mean much unless you actually sell your shares and go through the entire selling transaction.

REALIZED AND UNREALIZED GAINS OR LOSES—EXAMPLE

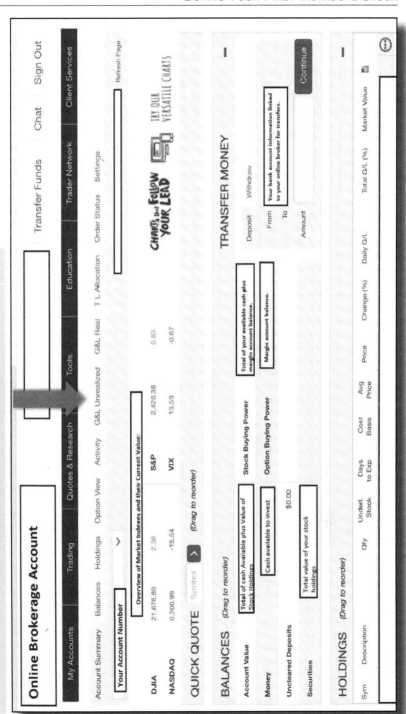

Once you decide to sell your investment, that is when it turns into a "realized" gain or loss which means precisely that—it now became REAL. If you actually made a profit from a stock you sold, the money will sit in your account until you decide to use it for something else. If you sold the investment at a loss—you'll notice your account decrease by the corresponding dollar amount.

Also, remember that every time you complete a "sell" transaction (just like with the "buy), the online broker will charge a transaction fee. It can be $4.95, $6.95, or $0 depending on the online broker or investing account you are using.

Because there is a significant difference between "realized" and "unrealized" gains or loses, it doesn't make any sense to panic when the stock market is going through one of its random downturns. If you still believe in the stock(s) you purchased and nothing has fundamentally changed about the business, you can choose to leave things alone until the market "recovers" again. If you decide to panic and actually sell things, your loses become real.

The challenge comes when you are actually making money from your investments and are trying to decide if you want to turn "unrealized" gains into "realized." The fact of the matter is that the stock market is unpredictable and no one has a crystal ball. Those investments you own might continue going up in price or something might happen that causes a drop in the price.

As the "manager" of your own self-directed investing account, you'll always need to make a decision on what course of action to take with the holdings in your portfolio.

Speaking of selling your investments, let's explore some scenarios where this is something you might seriously consider.

Deciding When To SELL

The decision of "when" to sell a stock you own is a difficult one for many—regardless of the level of investing experience.

On a personal level, although I've held onto 90% of my investments for years, there have been times that I have made the decision to sell, but not without some serious analysis of the situation.

Something that can help you tremendously in the future when you are confronted with whether or not to sell a stock you own, is making sure that you write out a solid investing thesis for everything you buy ahead of time.

You can come up with a clear and concise investing thesis once you complete your research of a particular stock and decide that you do want to buy it. The strategy of having a thesis will help in your decision-making process when a stock you own is going through struggles, and you're trying to decide what to do.

There is no reason to get overly complicated when creating an investing thesis. You can simply ask yourself a few questions:

- What is the **CORE** reason why I am buying this stock?

- Under what future circumstances would I consider selling?

- What would be a "deal breaker"?

If after reviewing your initial answers to those questions you realize that nothing has changed about your thesis, you'll think twice before selling and might have an easier time keeping emotions out of your decision.

You should always know WHY you bought something in the first place. If that reason changes in a way that doesn't sit well with you, and you see those changes negatively reflected in the stock price, it might be a good idea to think seriously about whether you should move on.

The point of investing is to let your money compound over many years. If nothing has changed about your original thesis, you can allow the stock to go through its temporary fluctuations. Remember that all businesses go through ups and down and it is a natural part of any business cycle. At the end of the day, the choice will always be yours.

Other reasons why you might consider selling can include:

- You realize there is a better stock or investment where you can put your money, so you might sell all or some of your position in a particular stock to allocate to something else.

- You bought a stock that has significantly appreciated in value, and you'd like to cash out some of that money to invest in something else.

- You are going through a significant life change—perhaps getting married, buying a home, kids enter the picture, starting a business, retiring, etc., and you'd like to use the money.

Ideally, if you can just leave your investments alone, it might be better to do just that. The decision on what to do with the stocks and investments you own will ultimately always be yours.

Step #3:

Keep an eye on your investments (while staying sane)

Something you might start to wonder as you begin your investing journey is how often you should be looking at your investing accounts. Some people like to know how their stocks are doing at all times and they might log into their accounts multiple times per day. Other people are more relaxed about it and might just leave things alone and only check from time to time.

While there is no "right or wrong" approach to how often you should be checking your investing accounts—I want to remind you, as I have noted multiple times, that the stock market is very unpredictable and volatile in the short term. One week you might notice all your stocks are doing amazing, and the next week the market as a whole might be falling apart.

The ongoing fluctuations are part of the ebbs and flow of how the markets work. There is no need to be watching your portfolios daily and freaking out whenever a downturn comes.

One strategy you can use to keep informed about any news related to the stocks you own without having to log into your investment accounts is to set alerts on Google News or Yahoo! Finance for specific companies you want to keep track of.

You can also take a look at your stocks whenever they report quarterly earnings (every 3 months) just to check on their performance.

Besides that, you can check the actual account maybe every couple of weeks or monthly.

I want to warn you about logging into your investing accounts during the days in which you know the market is going through some type of downturn or rough patch. You might be tempted to sell or take action based on emotion. This is rarely—if ever—a good idea.

The only reason I log into my investing accounts during days in which the stock market is going through a rough patch, is to purchase a stock I've been wanting to buy at a discount. Otherwise, I go on about my life and occupy myself in other things.

When you are investing for the long term—**years** not days—temporary fluctuations in the markets should be expected and not cause unnecessary panic.

Part IV:
Important Things to Know

*The point of diversification
is that you should NEVER
have all your money
in one single investment
because anything can happen.
Being well diversified can
significantly lower your risk
if any stock in your portfolio
is going through a temporary
downturn. Ideally, you want
the rest of your portfolio
to make up for any weaknesses.*

What It Means to Invest "On Margin"

We briefly mentioned margin investing toward the end of the section on online brokerage accounts. However, it is important we elaborate more on what this means.

When you open a self-directed investing account and depending on how much money you fund your account with, you might be given the option to open a "Margin Account."

For the majority of online brokers, you are only given this option if you deposit $2,000 or more of your own money (this is known as your cash account). However, the minimal requirement for margin accounts can vary depending on the investing platform you are using.

In simple terms, buying on margin means that you are using borrowed money that the online broker lends you to invest. As with any loan, the option to accept a margin account and subsequently use it means there are interest rates involved (some as high as 9%), as well as repayment guidelines.

One of the most important things to keep in mind is that you will be responsible for paying back the loan **regardless** of whether or not you make money on your investments. This can get messy and is extremely risky.

In the margin world, your stocks or investments are collateral for that "loan." If things go south and you end up losing money on your finances to the point that the online broker wants their loan back (usually when your losses are close to exceeding what you borrowed), the online broker will want to recover their loan immediately.

Some brokers will give you a limited time to deposit additional cash into your cash account to cover your margin loan. However, if this is not done, one of the things they can do is go ahead and sell your shares without any warning to cover their own assets.

The way most online brokers make money is by charging you a transaction fee when you buy and sell stocks. However, another way they make money is through the interest gained through your deposits and by offering a margin account.

Therefore, it makes sense that they would want to protect their funds and will be watching your account like a hawk to make sure you are not in danger of defaulting on your loan.

The market can be risky and volatile in the short term and we just never really know what will happen from one day to the next. You never want to be in a position where not only does your investment do poorly, and you end up losing tons of money, but also realize you owe money plus interest to your broker.

When it comes to investing, the peace of mind that comes from buying and selling stocks using your own money is priceless. You do not have to worry about anything other than waiting for your own money to grow and compound over time.

Even if some of your investments do poorly, at least you know there's no one else's money involved, and you can be at peace with that.

Protecting Your Portfolio from Volatility & Risk:

The Power of Diversification

You might recall that at the very beginning of this book, under the "Before We Get Started" section, I talked about the risk that come with stock investing.

One way in which you can protect your portfolio from the risk, volatility, and unpredictability is to be well diversified.

Diversification means that you are invested in different things and are not putting all of the money you have available for investing in "one basket" or one single stock.

The definition of diversification can mean different things to different people.

Diversification can mean:

- Building a portfolio that is made up of stocks from various companies covering different industries and sectors.

- Having a mix of index funds, ETFs, REITs, and bonds.

- Building a portfolio with stocks, ETFs, and Index Funds.

The possibilities can be quite broad!

I'd also like to note that cash should also be part of any healthy diversified portfolio. Cash means money that sits in your account and hasn't been invested. This can come in handy for when you want to take advantage of some investing opportunities or to have a cushion there for when you need it.

The point of diversification is that you should NEVER have all your money in one single investment because anything can happen. Being well diversified can significantly lower your risk if any stock in your portfolio is going through a temporary downturn. Ideally, you want the rest of your portfolio to make up for any weaknesses.

While we all expect that every single company where we invest our money turns out to be a solid business that is profitable and thriving—we also have to prepare for when this is not the case. The expectation is that, through diversification, the return on investment that comes from the winners in your portfolio are substantial enough that they can cover any losses from the stocks that perhaps didn't perform as you expected them to.

Bottom line: Never have all your money in one single stock or investment and make sure you always choose quality so that your winners can more than cover your losers, if you ever have any.

Final Thoughts...

We've arrived at the end of the book. You should be extremely proud of yourself for your time and commitment to learning how to invest. I wish you a life filled with health, love, success, and a whole lot of profits!

If you have any questions about any of the topics covered in this guide, you can email me: Girlsonthemoney@gmail.com. You can also find me on social media. My Instagram handle is @Girlsonthemoney.

And remember—I teach everything I covered in this guide, plus a whole lot more, in my highly rated step-by-step investing course for beginners. To find out when the next class will begin, send me an email or head over to our blog: Girlsonthemoney.com/InvestingCourses.

Happy investing!

And remember ...

Photo credit: Vernée Norman <u>verneenormanstudios@gmail.com</u>

Made in the USA
Columbia, SC
19 July 2020